Get ahead; give a

Give a damn – the proceeds of this book all go to help people without a job or a home get back into work – how to be more effective and successful at work – and keep your sanity

The whole amount you paid for this book will directly help people with mental health problems who are struggling to get both a job and somewhere to live – people who desperately want to get back on their feet and have a 'normal' life again. Thank you.

Contact Rachael Stock, The Have a Job; Give A Damn Project,
c/o Pearson Education, 128 Long Acre, London WC2E 9AN
Email: hajgad@pearsoned-ema.com

The costs of this book project were underwritten by
Pearson plc, and neither Pearson nor Waterstones are
receiving any financial benefit from the book sales.
See p. 57 for acknowledgements.

give a

"When you're
in alligators
remember tha
exercise is to

ii

Your work is swamp draining. The alligators are the obstacles to you doing your work effectively and achieving great success. This book contains a collection of practical ideas, thoughts and suggestions from leading career and personal skills authors that will help you overcome the problem people and situations (alligators) in your life, and find greater success and satisfaction at work.

damn

up to your arse
t's difficult to
he object of the
drain the swamp."

 Help yourself get ahead...

Leading homelessness agencies estimate that there are approximately 400,000 people homeless in England today. A high proportion of these people have mental health problems.

Over a third of hostel dwellers and 60% of night shelter and day-centre users have some form of psychiatric problem (Office for National Statistics, 1998). This compares with 5% of the general population. Mental health problems, such as depression, psychosis and personality disorders, can affect people's ability to live independently, and often are a major factor in a person becoming homeless. Additionally, people who have become homeless due to a crisis in the family, leaving care, the loss of a job or the breakdown of a relationship are more exposed to the type of stress that can lead to a serious deterioration in their mental health.

HOW ARE YOU HELPING?

Homeless people with a history of mental health problems have specific education and training needs. **Off the Streets and into Work** has found that one-to-one intensive guidance and support raises the levels of confidence and self-esteem that are crucial for this group as they progress into work or education. The money you spent on this book will fund and support "learning coaches" to deliver this much-needed service.

contents

contents

introduction

What would be the ideal job? For most of us, probably one where you enjoy what you do, where you feel valued, where you use your talents, you work in a positive and supportive environment with people you like, and where you are stretched – but not stressed.

Do you feel like that? Then you're probably achieving a lot at work and in life. Happy, fulfilled, stretched (but supported) people achieve the most at work and get the most from life. They drain a lot of swamps – and have a good time doing it.

However, most of us face a few alligators… those subversive obstacles that get in the way of a productive, high-achieving but low-stress kind of life. Some of them we create ourselves, some of them are placed there by other people and some of them ARE other people. Some of them just are.

This book will help you achieve more and be more successful by suggesting ways in which you can deal with (or avoid) the alligators and get back to the enjoyable business of swamp draining. At the same time, by buying this book you are helping other people who, for one reason or another, haven't had a job at all for a while and are struggling to get back on the ladder to a normal job and normal life.

Everybody involved in this book believes in one thing – that it *is* possible to have a job and give a damn – and we hope that you will find big personal success and, at he same time, discover your own way to make life better for somebody else.

Carmel McConnell

You're more in control than you think

You have a lot more control over most work/life situations than you might think.

This said, chances are when you are faced with your own life and your own personal swamp that needs draining, you probably don't feel very in control. Areas of powerlessness in life you might be aware of include lottery numbers getting drawn, your footie team winning, paying off bills, and your career generally. OK, the first two are hard to influence. But your life is, against all those long-held beliefs, something you *can* do something about – improve even.

"...your life is, against all those long-held beliefs, something you can do something about – improve even."

Before we start looking at all the ways you can change your life for the better, it's worth having a bit of a think about what it means to be in control of your life. You've got to believe you are in control enough to make changes happen.

WHAT DOES "IN CONTROL" LOOK LIKE?

Well, that depends on you. If you feel stressed when you haven't got the overnight bag packed at least two weeks before a weekend in the sun, by all means plan ahead.

Similarly if you're unable to see a deadline unless at least two extensions have passed, there is no point talking about a schedule and active forward planning. So before we go on, it's worth having a quick think about who you are.

SO, WHO ARE YOU?

1. When you have a piece of work to do by next week, do you:
a) Research, do it, review it this week to get it finished.
b) Forget when next week, feel guilty around Wednesday and do it two days late.
c) Something in between.

2. When your dinner arrives cold and wrong in a nice restaurant, do you:
a) Re-read the *Best Thai in Glasgow Guide*, complain and then sue the owners.
b) Write it off as a dud restaurant, forget the food and have another beer.
c) Something in between.

3. Your parents are coming over for Sunday lunch. Do you:
a) Phone and ask them to suggest a menu, then shop and cook the night before.
b) Hope you can hear the doorbell when they arrive, because you had a large Saturday night.
c) Something in between.

Get ahead; give a damn

Mostly As – you are going to need more data, more facts, more schedules and probably enough time on your own to balance the chaos of other people. Also maybe more tolerance of friends who feel differently about these things (and if my sister is reading this, please let me off sometime, OK?).

Mostly Bs – you are going to need to be free, to roam the week without deadlines if possible and with maximum chance to hang out with other wonderful people and talk about ideas (without needing to make anything happen necessarily). You also need to not mess people about, which sometimes happens because you forget that other people have lives that matter too. (If my sister is reading this, I am sorry and I will replace it.)

Mostly Cs – you are strangely balanced – and I hope you can be honest and say what your real end of the spectrum is. Otherwise you are doing OK on the in-control stakes. (By the way, my sister and I could use some coaching on how you do it!)

Where are you? Being in control will be different according to your natural preference.

Thankfully we are not generic humans, so I would ask that you please take all advice in this chapter and filter it in the context of who you are.

HOW CAN YOU TELL IF YOU ARE IN CONTROL?

Behaviour is one way. External actions show the level of internal control, if you like. What are behaviours?

Our behaviours are defined as visible actions (conscious and unconscious) seen by friends, families and colleagues – oh, and alligators of course.

Are you in control of your behaviour?

Mostly, apart from:

a) during certain underwater situations with 'gator teeth within flossing distance

b) in any negotiation with someone who has power over your salary

c) when you're 55 minutes late to teach on your first Time Management event

d) when the Beckhams visit.

If we are talking about having *enough control*, not 100% control, then what does enough control look like?

- Enough control is when you are able to steer the day's events ahead of time.
- Enough control doesn't require telling any lies to anyone.
- Enough control is when you feel you can speak up for yourself and be honest.
- Enough control is when you feel you can handle it.
- Enough control is when you create different options.
- Enough control is when you sleep well.
- Enough control is when you don't need booze or another drug to get through the day.
- Enough control doesn't have any panic attached.
- Enough control is when you don't mind your flat being a

bit upside down, because deep down everything is OK.
- Enough control is when you eat (not over-eat, not under-eat) when you are hungry.
- Enough control is when you can ask for help, and be OK when someone actually helps.

WHY I CAN PROVE I'M NOT IN CONTROL

There are a few big myths in this area, which turn out to be big *myth-stakes*.

Myth 1: I don't know what I want to do. Even if I did, I couldn't do it. So I'll settle for this. I'm not in control of getting my ideal job.

Very few people do exactly what they want to do in the early stages of working life. Most of us try stuff to find the thing that feels most right. So – wherever you work, there are things that you can do to picture yourself in a place of greater control. Think about it. **You are more in control than you think…**

" *Being 100% in control is a lovely but unattainable goal.* "

Myth 2: I'm in debt so I can't do anything with my life right now. It's not in my control.

What if I were to suggest you are more in control because you are in debt. What?! The facts are: a) someone has deemed you creditworthy, which means you probably are because banks ain't charities (so someone has seen your potential even if it isn't you, at this moment); and b) you have to clear it, and the chances are that en route you'll be forced to learn and do stuff you wouldn't otherwise do.

If you are in debt, big time, do a weekly breakdown of where it goes and how much you need to pay off by when. Don't think a lack of cash changes everything – it doesn't change your ability to think, love, exercise, and show the world your talents. If it takes five years at £10 per week, so be it, and you are making progress, so just do that and you'll be fine.

Unless you want debt to be a big security blanket to stop you trying stuff. Is it?

Myth 3: I have to be totally in control of my ways/work/wardrobe/waistline/ because others seem to be able to do it.
Being 100% in control is a lovely but unattainable goal. No one is. So, right now, simply junk the idea of being totally on

Prioritising

Look at what is worth controlling in your life, then how to do it. At the same time you can chuck things that are not easy to control and/or yield small personal benefit, even if you do control them. If it works properly you will find the week frees up.

The very act of prioritising will prove, even to you, that you are more in control than you think. And the swamp will drain so much easier.

Swamp drainage

top of everything. It ain't possible, and that way madness lies. What is needed is enough control over enough things in your life. That way happiness lies.

Myth 4: I'm pretty crap at most things, so why bother?

Self-esteem and control. A joined-at-birth kind of link. For example, what if you hate your job, but you feel too bad about yourself to do anything?

Chances are you know you need to do something, but just can't face it. Times of low self-esteem happen to everyone, at different times. It is a cycle I have regularly fallen into. How can you tell? Feeling tired, unable to speak up, bored, vaguely annoyed, and wasting time. There are tactics to deal with this:

Tactic 1 Figure out what you enjoy doing. The best way to get back in control is to take the pressure off and take pleasurable action – do some small things that you like to do. Little by little get the circulation going again. Talk to someone about how you feel, read about someone you admire, take an hour to yourself and fill it with things you really enjoy.

Tactic 2 Look back over the past year and remember one time you were really happy. Remember it as if you were there now. Feel it – those times will come back.

Tactic 3 Now, when you are feeling a bit different, what one thing could you do that would make you feel a little more in control? Do it, for half an hour. Stop. Repeat…

Self-esteem changes after you take action, not before… Action first. Then you feel better. Funny that.

Myth 5: If I haven't got everything worked out in my mind about what I want to do, I'll fail.

No, that's not true either. Let's just say that if you want to make the workplace swamp a lovely place to thrive, your first task is to believe that your career and indeed whole life is all about transition. From here to somewhere happier, better – and whatever else you want. Sunnier? Richer? Full of the sounds of workplace crocodiles leaving? Fine.

Success is simply what you love doing; being done with/for people you know will gain some real benefit as a result. Being a little in control and able to steer is useful, but not essential. Yes, I realise that is not what it says in all the big management books, but it is true. Being in control means enough control over enough things, tuning your thinking into what makes you happy and taking care of the basics such as living on something other than toasted cheese sarnies.

Myth 6: People just take my day over. I can't control it.

Those actions that we file under "just the way it is" are very capable of being altered. For example, say Ms Understood in the Bristol office is forever emptying her whole sorry life story onto your virtual shoulder every time you prise time from the day for your tired old self. She has a homing instinct for your free five: "Sorry to bother you, have you got a minute?". Bam – there goes making plans for tonight. And that's just the way it is. Right? Or the fact that the new manager they've brought in is always in meetings and never available to see you, and you need to get your budget signed off. That's life.

Well no. The payoff for the call might be feeling like a good person by listening, or you can be a victim "I couldn't get Ms Understood off the phone". Change the payoff and you change your sense of being in control. Your big satisfaction can be saying "I'd really like to talk to you again about that, but right now I am finishing x y z, so can I call you back when I'm finished?". Not rude, just honest. As for Mr Budget, well, maybe you feel a bit sheepish about the extra padding you've put in there for stuff that you know deep down you can't justify. Take a bit out, then it'll be signed off this week because then you won't dread the chat? Why not?

All I know is that you can look back on years of not quite dealing with stuff and feel defeated, angry and a bit teary after a few tequilas. Or you can work out the most healthy payoff (getting stuff done and out the door at a reasonable time is one) for your actions. Try looking at the swamp and the 'gators again now. You *are* more in control than you think.

Carmel McConnell is the author of *Change Activist – Make Big Things Happen Fast* and *Soultrader – Find Purpose and You'll Find Success*. She is also the co-author of *Careers Un-Ltd* with Jonathan Robinson. All are published by momentum.

Dealing with problems before they start:
the art of alligator avoidance

Even when you have some semblance of control over your life, to get ahead at work you have to deal with the alligators – those nagging problems and tricky people situations that make it really very difficult to get on with your work effectively. But how much better would it be if the alligators didn't exist in the first place? How much easier would life be if your work was draining a reptile-free swamp?

There are a few simple principles and practices that, when integrated into your daily life, keep alligators at bay or prevent them from gathering to reach critical mass, and leave you to get on with whatever it is you'd really rather be doing. And so much less stressful too.

ALLIGATOR AVOIDANCE MADE EASY
Get things straight from the start

Work is often about avoiding blame and distributing it to other people when things go wrong. Things go wrong generally because they've started out wrong and the reason for that is that people haven't agreed what should happen in the first place. Deciding what you expect of someone and what they expect of you in any given situation is the best form of controlling and managing that situation. Set the mutual expectations before you start anything.

If I expect you to call me every day, you know exactly how to keep me happy, i.e. by calling me every day. You also know that I will be unhappy if that doesn't happen and once you fail to call me every day I can point out that we both agreed on this point and something must have changed for you to be failing to live up to our expectations. You can't complain that you didn't know I was expecting a daily call because we've already agreed what's expected. Agreeing things first makes managing them easier later.

" ...people need to be re-charmed every time you meet them. "

Put people at their ease

It is a real gift to be able to make total strangers feel at ease because naturally we're all wary of strangers. Smiling, listening, self-deprecation and a pinch of flattery are the keys and people who can employ these at will are said to be charming. Charm is a great word from the last century, a word which implies some kind of oil-based preparation in the hair, but charm is the ultimate business facilitator. As someone rather charming once said, "Charm is getting the answer 'yes' before you've even asked the question."

With people we work with over a period of time, familiarity encourages relaxation, but people need to be re-charmed every time you meet them. You know you've got a friend rather than a business relationship when you've banked enough of this relaxation and charm to be a grumpy old sod once in a while. The fastest way to put someone at ease is to make them feel superior. You can do this by admitting you're stupid or sad or unlucky. But the fastest way by far is to bang your head quite hard against a low beam. This instantly robs you of dignity, composure and intelligence and makes virtually anybody else look as though they've got their life together.

Avoid upsetting people

The most efficient way to get something done in the office is to have said thank you to everybody the last time. If you're the sort of person who dumps on people at the last moment, screams for results and then doesn't give a word of thanks, you'll find it gets increasingly difficult to get anything done,

" The most efficient way to get something done in the office is to have said thank you to everybody the last time. "

because everyone will glue your stuff to the bottom of their in-tray. It won't help your case either if the first time you've bothered to speak to a person is when you're dumping a massive amount of work on them. You need to have put in the spadework a long time before.

Ask people what they think about things

The most sincere form of flattery is to give someone your undivided attention. This gives them a very clear signal that you think they are worth listening to. Most people actually have strong opinions about how they could do their job better and how you could work together better. Most people are also deeply wary that they won't be listened to and that their opinions are of no account.

Be diplomatic

The quickest way to upset someone in the office is not to value their work. Here are a few good examples of this.

- When they've prepared a 50 minute presentation, ask them to present it in five.
- Get together a working party on their specialist subject and don't include them.
- Have a team celebration and don't ask them along because their job is so basic they don't really count.
- Ask them to do something and then tell them how to do it in minute detail.
- Ask them to do some extra work and then don't use it.
- Ask them why their job hasn't been done away with yet.

Alligators

Very often if you ask someone about their job and how they do it, you will learn something of use for the way you do your job and also for the way you can work more effectively with that person. Plus the very act of listening and acting on what you've heard is a powerful cement for your relationship.

Be aware, however, that there are a sizeable number of people who don't think but do like to talk, which they assume is the same thing. These people have one or two opinions which they've worked hard at, polished up and relish the opportunity to trot out. Occasionally, take a deep breath and give them the opportunity to do so, but try to have an exit strategy on hand in case they are on a continuous loop and start repeating everything.

Never get personal unless it's personal
Occasionally people will conspire against you in the office because they are a nasty piece of work and because they can't stand other people showing the initiative and confidence that they sorely lack. The natural temptation is to react in a similar nasty fashion. Don't. It's inevitable that throughout life you will meet people who don't like you and don't want to help you. In normal life you can just avoid these people and be on your way. In business you often can't avoid them; they may well be your boss.

" ...the one road you don't want to go down is making it personal. "

There are ways to manage this situation, but the one road you don't want to go down is making it personal. As soon as you make it personal for them you make it personal for you and you allow the places that matter to you, such as your dignity, self-respect, confidence and happiness, to be exposed to their attack. As hard as it may seem, you must do everything in your power to treat these people in a professional manner.

Very, very occasionally, even in our caring, sharing, coaching new world of work you will find yourself in a position where the personal and malicious actions of another individual threaten your livelihood, your health and, by extension, your nearest and dearest. You then have two options. Get a job somewhere else or confront the problem personally. Once you have chosen this second course you have to strike hard, strike quickly and sustain the attack until your opponent is rendered completely harmless. Generally, you'll be dealing with bullies and if you show bullies any weakness they will exploit it.

Follow the above principles, and you'll be much more likely to operate in an alligator-free zone. In which case, you're free to get on with achieving some useful and highly impressive swap draining.

SWAMP DRAINING MADE EASY
Get organised before you get an organiser
Working smarter not harder doesn't mean the application of more and better technology. It is more important that you yourself work efficiently. Before you get a personal organiser, get yourself personally organised. If you're clear in your own mind about what is useful, important and what is mission-critical data, then you can cut a clear swathe through the information clutter that surrounds us all.

It's easy to think that by working later at the office you give yourself permission to start work later. In reality that is not how it works. Once you start getting in later in the day, it has a knock-on effect and you find yourself losing more and more time as the day goes on. Starting early, on the other hand, gets you ahead of the game and makes it easier for you to stay ahead. Remember, it's always easier to prepare for a meeting before it than after it.

Take control of your time

Keep control of your own diary. Especially resist the urge to fill all your own white spaces. If you're nervous about opening your diary in front of friends or colleagues and for them to get snow-blindness because your days are so empty, then just fill them in with all the things you're going to think about or do yourself. Add a name and a time and everyone will think you've got back to back meetings (the Holy Grail of workaholics and the perfect recipe for ulcers and general unhappiness). Don't put things in your diary unless they absolutely have to go in.

Alligators

Be enthusiastic or confident or both

Life can be a lot like a sponsored bike ride. In general people will go out of their way to back people with enthusiasm, especially for a cause that seems well founded and well thought out. And don't forget, enthusiasm doesn't mean talking in tongues and emitting a strange aura of light; it means communicating to others that you are happy and inspired by something worth doing and that they would also be a help and inspiration to you.

In business, the difference between people who become directors of large companies (their own or others) and those who don't often boils down to nothing more exciting than confidence: the confidence in their own abilities and the corresponding confidence they inspire in others. Confidence is actually more important than ability. There are many examples in business of people whose supreme self-belief has carried them unscathed from one monstrous cock-up to another. They get away with this because their confidence is so rock solid that they simply can't believe that any mistakes could possibly be anything to do with them. Similarly, all their shareholders and employees believe the same.

Talk to people with experience

Arrogant people don't talk to people with experience because they worship at the altar of their own intelligence. Intelligent people do talk to people with experience because it's a fantastic way of helping yourself to knowledge and avoiding big pitfalls. When you talk to people with experience, you're not just listening to what they have to say, you're also telling them what you have to say and gaining supporters along the way. Remember, people are generally happy to help, they just need to be asked.

However, when you're listening to people with experience you should only listen with one ear open. That's because everyone's experience is different and what worked yesterday won't necessarily work tomorrow. Also, people with experience are talking from memory, and the memory is a very efficient PR department, creating myths and polishing the truth so that over the years, events and decisions become almost unrecognisable from what really happened.

Under-promise and over-deliver

Everything in life is relative. If I ask you out for dinner at a restaurant and we go for a kebab, then you're likely to think I've over-promised and under-delivered and our working relationship will have been damaged. If I've promised you a kebab (not a recommended business practice) and taken you for a slap-up feed in the *Manoir de la Grande Addition* then I will have under-promised and over-delivered and our business relationship will be strengthened. The point is that everyone judges results by their expectation of results. If you're the favourite and you come second you've done badly, if you're a no-hoper and you come second, you've done well.

In the office, the trick is to set manageable expectations of delivery. These should always err on the cautious side without being uncompetitive. You don't want to use under-promising like the railways use it: making journey times ever longer in the timetables in order to cover up weaker and weaker performance. Instead you want to set expectations at a level where they can be met 80–90% of the time, with the final 10–20% of times exceeding expectations. This gives you the double benefit of always being seen to deliver on target and often to be delivering above and beyond targets. Over-promise and you will consistently fail to meet the target and often be way below it.

Define your goals and stick to them

Without a set of goals and a clear direction in your work, you're never going to know whether you're working effectively or not. Without clear goals you won't know when to say "yes" to opportunities and when to say "no" to work that is irrelevant. Knowing what you want makes it easier to avoid always doing what other people want.

As you work your goals may shift. This is because working and gaining knowledge and experience often illuminates and defines your goals more clearly. It's not necessarily a sign of weakness if you change your goals either. Over the course of life your goals change naturally; the key thing is to feel some sort of purpose and direction to what you're doing.

What you must avoid doing is ditching your goals as soon as the going becomes tough. All the good things in life and the things worth doing are difficult to achieve. They require the continuous application of intelligent and directed effort. Unless, of course, you've made it your goal to pick the low-hanging fruit of life. Just be aware that a lot of other people also take the same approach and there is a limited amount of low-hanging fruit.

Guy Browning is the author of the modern work survival guide *Innervation* (momentum). He is also author of the management classic *Grass Roots Management – How to Grow Initiative and Responsibility in all your People*, and of the highly humorous *Weak at the Top – A Year in the Life of the Last Cavemanager* (Prentice Hall Business).

Dealing with difficult people:
combatting the worst kind of alligator

3

It's very unlikely, even if you follow all the alligator avoidance tips in Chapter 2 with absolute dedication and assiduousness, that you will ever occupy a completely alligator-free zone. So, you need to know how to deal with them when they appear.

Possibly the worst kind of alligator is the "difficult" person: most of our worst stresses and problems would evaporate if it weren't for difficult people. You'll be pleased to know that there are certain underlying techniques which, once learnt, you can apply to most difficult people. Yes, it does take a short time to learn them initially, but the investment is worth it. These techniques will help you resolve a host of problems with such ease you will barely notice there *was* a problem.

" ...anger is rarely the best way for anyone to get what they want. "

There are certain types of tricky behaviour that almost anyone can exhibit – your boss, colleagues, direct reports and even customers and suppliers. Some people exhibit them regularly and some only occasionally. Whichever is the case, they can come at you out of the blue, so you need to be ready to deflect them instantly. That way, you can resolve the problem swiftly and permanently.

TRICKY BEHAVIOURS

So what are these behaviours? The key ones, which I'm sure you'll recognise, are:

- anger
- silence
- emotional blackmail.

ANGER

People are occasionally justified in getting angry – we all are from time to time. But people who lose their temper in order to bludgeon you into giving in to them are a different matter. The worst thing you can do is to let them get away with it. If it works, they'll keep doing it to you, and everyone else.

The first thing you need to do is to brush up on your assertiveness skills. You'll need them. You mustn't allow yourself to be intimidated, and you're not paid to be shouted at by someone who has never grown up. Here are a few tips:

- Don't allow yourself to be shouted or ranted at. Be assertive and say something along the lines of, "I don't like being shouted at, and I shall leave/put down the phone if you don't calm down."

- If they continue, do just that: leave or put the phone down. Say "I'll talk to you when you've calmed down", or, if you find that hard to say, just say "Excuse me" and make your exit.

- Continue this response at any subsequent encounters where they get angry, until they learn to talk to you rationally and reasonably.

SILENCE

People sulk because they want to let you know how upset they are. If they didn't sulk (they feel) you would think the matter wasn't important to them. Almost all of us are prone to sulk occasionally, but some people do it over such seemingly minor issues that it ends up happening frequently and creates an unpleasant and unhelpful attitude that can seriously sour the working relationship. Whether you are dealing with a regular sulker or an unexpected dose of the silent treatment, the guidelines for handling it are the same.

- Silence is intended to make you feel guilty once you realise how upset the person is. Any approach to handling a sulker only works if you honestly have nothing to feel guilty about. So when you have the kind of discussion with this person that can lead to an unpleasant silence, make sure you genuinely listen to them with an open mind, explain the reasons behind your view of the matter, and act in a friendly and reasonable way. Once the discussion is over, if they then still choose to sulk you know that there was nothing else you could have done except give in for no good reason, simply to avoid the sulking.

- The aim is that you will capitulate. Never, ever do so. If it works for them once, they will try it every time.

- Don't perpetuate the atmosphere by being short with them either. Behave as if everything were normal. If they give you the silent treatment, just say "OK, we'll sort it out later". If it really can't wait, force them to answer you. Ask them the question and then wait for their response. And wait... and wait. Force them to break the silence by answering – it's their turn to speak, after all. Once you've shown them that you can hold out longer than them, they won't try that technique again.

EMOTIONAL BLACKMAIL

"I'm going to be in a real mess if you don't help me out with this." "Don't give me a hard time for being late; I find it so difficult to get up in the mornings." "Please don't be unco-operative." Emotional blackmail is a popular weapon for

Keep a lid on it

Never respond to anger with anger. It doesn't work, it inflames the situation, it makes a resolution to the problem far less likely, it stores up resentment and bad feeling, and it loses you the moral high ground. So bite your tongue before you're tempted to bite their head off.

Alligators

getting people to do whatever the blackmailer wants. They are playing on your guilt, or your desire to be popular, in order to manipulate you into doing things their way.

But there's one thing you need to know about emotional blackmail: it doesn't work on assertive people. And the emotional blackmailers learn to recognise assertive people and they stop using this insidious technique on them. So apply a bit of assertiveness and become impervious to this kind of manipulation.

- Recognise emotional blackmail for what it is. As soon as you start to feel guilty about saying no, or emotionally uncomfortable about your response to someone, ask yourself "Am I being emotionally blackmailed?" Once you're alert to the possibility, you'll have no trouble recognising when it's happening.
- Tell yourself that emotional blackmail is not a fair, equal, adult behaviour, and that you owe nothing to those who use it. If they're prepared to use such an underhand approach with you, you are quite entitled to respond by not giving in to it.
- Now simply stand your ground. If they persist, adopt the stuck record technique. Don't allow them to make you feel bad – it is they who are behaving unreasonably, not you.
- Challenging people directly over this technique can cause unpleasantness, but with some people you may find that you can say – with a joke and a laugh – "Careful! That's starting to sound like emotional blackmail…" It pulls them up short. If they think you're getting wise to them they'll back off.

TRICKY TYPES OF DIFFICULT PEOPLE

Some people have a particular characteristic that drives you mad, and makes your job harder. So here's a guide to handling a few of the most difficult people you're likely to encounter.

The moaner

People who moan all the time just bring you down. Their negative attitude is contagious. You can't change their personality, but you can anticipate and prevent a lot of the whingeing.

- Try to avoid putting them under pressure – this almost always leads this type of person to complain.
- Before they complain, ask them if they need any help. Occasionally they may see this as an invitation to complain, but more often than not they will tell you things are fine (if they'd thought of a complaint they'd have voiced it already). Once they have committed themselves to the attitude that everything's OK it makes it harder for them to start moaning later.
- When they complain, these people are prone to keep analysing the reasons why the problem has arisen. Focus them on the solution instead. "Well, it's happened now. What do you think is the best way to resolve it?" Just occasionally it may be useful to know the background so you can prevent the problem recurring, but even so, suggest to them "Let's identify the reason for the situation later; for now, let's just worry about resolving it."

The know-all

Know-alls are infuriating. You find yourself wanting them to be wrong even though the project and the team will suffer – and that's not healthy. But how do you stop them frustrating everyone?

- Know-alls are incapable of saying "I was wrong". Rather than pointing out their errors, ask them to explain their plans to you so that they can spot their own mistakes as they speak. If they don't identify them, ask questions that focus on the area you feel needs closer scrutiny.
- Don't try to humiliate them in front of other people – tempting though it is – you will only antagonise them.
- Give them credit where it's due, but make them share it: "That was a very good idea, Pat. Mind you, we'd never have got the results we did from it without Jason's inspired planning. And Jacky's presentation was first class." Make sure the know-all recognises everyone else's contribution as well as their own.

The prima donna

It's no coincidence that these people are prone to act like five year olds. This kind of behaviour is usually learned in early childhood; they discover that by creating a scene they can get what they want. In a work environment, however, you want people to focus on what is the best way to achieve the team's objectives, not on fulfilling their personal agenda.

- The prima donna has learnt that this kind of behaviour gets them what they want. All you have to do is teach them that it doesn't – at least not here. It may take time after years of finding it successful, but if you're consistent they'll learn in the end.
- Don't respond to this kind of behaviour. Find an excuse to leave the room – to make a phone call or grab a

coffee – and come back when they've calmed down.
Be responsive and willing to listen as soon as they're
calm and rational, but opt out of the conversation
whenever they become childish.

- Don't meet their emotion with emotion of your own:
meet it with cool, objective, factual statements and
information-seeking questions.

The aggressive type

This type of person can upset other team members. Aggressive
people tend to think and act fast, and they are often insecure
and need recognition and personal power. These aspects of
their make-up can guide you in dealing with them.

- Because they like to get on with things, it eases your
relationship with them if you can move at their speed on
projects where you're working closely with them.
- They need recognition and will sometimes put people
down in order to make themselves appear superior. If you
give them credit when they deserve it they won't do this.
- Domineering people tend to try and shout other people
down. Don't react. If everyone else stays calm they will
start to look rather silly losing their cool. They'll soon
learn to stay in control rather than make a fool of
themselves.

The put-down merchant

These people like to belittle others by making snide remarks
or ones which contain poorly concealed criticisms. They are

full of remarks such as "Late again, Kate? No surprises there," or "You actually managed to read it, did you? Mind you, I don't imagine you understood much of it." If it's any consolation, other people aren't likely to take the implications seriously, since they will all be well aware of the type of person they're coming from. But how do you deal with it?

- The first thing is not to give them any ammunition. If you are always late, it's difficult to respond to the accusation, however unpleasantly they have chosen to put it. So make sure you give them no valid grounds for putting you down.
- If you rise to the bait, you will only create a row which will get you worse than nowhere. If you rile this person, they'll get worse, not better.
- If you respond submissively, on the other hand, you encourage them to carry on putting down you and other people. If you are happy to ignore the remarks with dignity you can do so, but if you want them to stop this isn't the way to go about it.

Assertiveness pays

Aggressive people don't necessarily want you to capitulate to them all the time – they often don't like people who are wet. They would much rather be able to respect you. So stand up to them assertively (but non-aggressively) when you need to.

Alligators

- So you're left with the rational centre course – assertiveness. Reply with a polite question which challenges the put-down. When they say, "Late again?", you reply "Apart from last Wednesday, when there was a tube strike, I don't believe I've been late for several months. Which occasion are you referring to?" This will take the wind out of their sails and you'll find, if you regularly employ this technique, they'll soon learn that if they try to belittle you, it's them who will end up looking foolish.

Ros Jay is the author of many career books, including *How to Manage Your Boss*; *Fast Thinking Manager's Manual*; *How to Get A Pay Rise*; *How to Build A Great Team* and *How to Handle Tough Situations at Work* (all published by Prentice Hall Business).

Building coalitions:
swamp drainage is a team sport

Work is a team sport. It can be anything from co-operation to emotional suffocation depending on your ability to manage it. Yes, your ability. The people you work with are a potentially great resource – for your career success.

Your work content might change, as might your physical location and place in the hierarchy, but the existence of some sort of team around you is a consistent feature of the things we do to earn a salary. (The only exceptions might be fine art, round-the-world solo yachting, or membership of a religious order. Or a combination, i.e. Sister Mary paints the view in pastels while sailing round the Cape of Good Hope. As a work of art, it ended up slightly more abstract than intended.)

" Think co-swamp drainers rather than alligators. "

This chapter is about using those who work in the same office, division or organisation as you as a resource. Think co-swamp drainers rather than alligators. You can achieve your goals, learn, try out new ideas, have fun (even) if your mindset changes to believe that your fellow employees are there to help. The alternative is choosing to resent the annoying people who hang around the place while you are trying to get some work done. Your call.

THE WORK PLACE

First some context. Places to work mirror the markets they serve. Where you are has a structure that reflects the environment in which you serve your customers. Let me explain – because it is important that you understand what drives the shape of the place you work in before you start shaping your personal career network.

Markets come in many forms, e.g. the global telecoms market, the local fruit & veg market, the internal ideas market where you work ("Did you see Steve's client report?"). Each of those markets has been through some rapid changes recently. People are offering services and products where they see the opportunity, not where they have history.

The market place has changed into a mass of small alliances, partnerships and joint ventures. The most successful teams mirror that. They add associates, use internal help, work strange hours, get more feedback, learn to listen. They are not fixed, hierarchical structures with everyone set in concrete job descriptions. Jobs are fluid, although annoyingly not until after 7pm.

Open your ears
Ask better quality open questions to get better quality open answers
– of yourself
– of colleagues
– of your customers.
Allow yourself to listen. Listening builds strong relationships.

Swamp drainage

BUILDING COALITIONS

Your work colleagues are an opportunity. "For what?" I hear your inner voice cry. Theft from bags under desks at lunchtime? A two-week romance forever regretted each time public small talk has to happen?

Well, no. You can choose to create a working environment which absolutely supports your career ambitions. Within some constraints, yes – I absolutely expect that there are some things even you cannot influence. Your board of directors. Probably not. Your product brand strategy. Probably not. Your overall scheduling of tasks and apportioning of dull work vs groovy stuff. Probably yes. Your chance to take on new projects where you can learn and grow. Probably yes. But before you can get to those, you have to have a few things in place. View these as a plan or a checklist.

How to build a career coalition where you work

1. Work out what the goal is. You can't build a coalition of swamp drainers if the draining of swamps hasn't been identified as the most important thing to do.
2. Accept that everyone will see the goal differently, depending on their view of the world. You see the goal as being to drain swamp one by Tuesday, because on Wednesday you go on holiday. Your colleagues stay on.
3. Make the time to check in with people, viewing the world with their eyes, even if it is a simple two-minute "how are you?". The most powerful market coalitions in the world of business are based on a five-minute

phone call once a month. "Hi, how are you. How are the kids? You still trying to finish that deal in Asia Pac? I'll give you a call if I get over there. Bye." This is apparently how CEOs stay linked to their network, – yes the ones that create multi-billion pound mergers. The networks are held together by simply staying in touch.

4. Recognise that everyone (including yourself) is doing their best. If they are not, there is probably a good reason.

5. Be honest in your relationships with team colleagues (e.g. do what you say you are going to do, consistently). A little fib can become a Big Secret amazingly quickly. A Big Secret can rear up and bite you even harder than a hungry alligator.

6. Identify the source of common purpose in the team and state it. "We are here today with the same goal, fellow swamp drainers." Does anyone state the goal clearly where you work? The big overwhelming priority? If not, this is a common cause of swamp-draining inefficiency.

7. Broaden the scope of discussions so that everyone can participate. Don't cut people out, because it hurts. "Carol and Simon, two of our new swamp drainers, are away on a swamp-draining course today – who is going to catch them up when they get back? Thank you."

8. Encourage others to shine (because you have learned that being given a chance, and importantly being given credit for a job well done, probably got you started on the road to success).

9. Mentally acknowledge that everyone is in transition to perfection, some further back down the road than others. This will help you let go of the desire to judge, blame and snipe (er – so what will you do with all that free time?).
10. Consciously aim to build trust with those around you.

INSPIRING OTHERS

If you don't have a happy team of swamp drainers around you, my view is you are at least partially responsible. If you are unhappy where you are working, and you say that is because of the people you work with, sorry to be in your face, but it is up to you to change it. Or find someplace better.

Leading from the middle

Leading the way with ideas makes formal hierarchies unimportant. If you are somewhere that allows you to speak, you can pitch ideas. If you find the microphone permanently turned off when it's your turn in the staff meeting, then consider whether your journey to career success is really taking the right path, right now.

Pulling people together

Remember – your boss is part of your team. OK. Let's take one scenario. Radical idea here – your boss as human. OK primate hybrid – let's say you work with a *harangue-utan* of a boss. No peace, constant demands, persistent requests and that's just the mobile phone calls on the way to work. This

boss is Enemy No. 1, right? There to make life less wonderful.
Maybe. I suspect that the *harangue-utan* is actually just
someone who has been where you are, got promoted,
doesn't like her life and has forgotten what it's like at your
level. What you need is a boss-realignment strategy (also
known as alligator acceptance) which goes like this:

Alligator acceptance

- Empathise in advance – spend a day in her moccasins.
- Ask better questions – open questions: "what if?" instead of "you git".
- Be personally accountable for making it work – you can change your
  thoughts about this person, even if you can't change the person.

Alligators

You might also need a team realignment strategy. Day one,
new job, and suddenly your work horizon is strewn with
smiling strangers who, between 9am and 6pm, become quasi-
family. Yes, in some cases including a quasi-modo. You start to
make assumptions and form opinions about these people.

So you look around you - what do you see right now? How
you view the people you work with has a massive effect on
how well the team operates. If you start seeing your team as
people who can help each other achieve something, it's quite
amazing how everything starts to improve. The difference
could be your attitude.

Carmel McConnell – *for Carmel's book details see p.9.*

Dealing with overload:
when the swamp fills up as fast as you drain it

Even if we take the alligators out of the equation, swamp draining can be a tough challenge by itself. Especially if it's a mighty big swamp you're trying to drain.

We all know the feeling: your boss dumps more and more work on you; you've got to do your colleagues' jobs as well as your own because they aren't doing them; you can't delegate (or is it won't?)… suddenly the swamp is filling faster than you can drain it and panic sets in.

WORK OVERLOAD AND STRESS

This doesn't make sense from your employers' perspective: overload causes stress, and 30 million working days are lost each year through stress, according to Professor Cary Cooper. And it certainly doesn't make sense for you: overload also causes negative feelings about your job, and that's seriously bad for your health. Male patients who answered negatively to enquiries about work were often found to be suffering from headaches, palpitations or sleeping difficulties. "This distress poses a much more significant threat to the physical and mental well-being of young men than virtually everything else combined," says Dr James LeFanu.

CAN'T SAY NO?

Doing too much is stressful – as is not having enough to do – and when you're overloaded you often sink deeper into the swamp instead of remembering you are there to drain it. But whose fault is it you've got too much to do? Could it be your own? You panic about recriminations, fear the boss's disapproval, worry about not keeping up with your peers and feel too exhausted to find the strength to be assertive. So, you say "OK" when you mean "No". You say "That's fine, I'll do that", when you mean "No way, I will explode if I'm given any more to do".

Know your limits

So how on earth do you deal with overload before you're submerged? The first and most critical step is to know your limits and communicate these clearly to your boss and other people. Sometimes you just have to say "No" and mean it. Sometimes you have to stand up for your rights and your self-respect and your health. We all find it simple to feed the alligators just for an easy life – but you don't have to be their breakfast.

Swamp drainage

If you have problems saying what you mean, think about what will happen if you don't set your limits and always say yes to that extra bit of work. Here are the possible outcomes:

- Things will get better all by themselves.
- Things will stay roughly the same.
- Things will get worse.

What do you think? Things will miraculously get better? Not in this swamp, matey. Things will stay the same? No way, it's always a downhill slide in muddy situations. Things will get worse? You've got it.

And what will happen to you? Will you suddenly find magic ways of coping? Of course not. Will you suddenly find another pair of hands? Not likely given the rate you're feeding them to the alligators. Will you discover another eight hours a day? Nope. What will happen is that you will get more and more stressed. Your health will suffer. Your home life will suffer.

So, time to regulate your workflow by saying no to tasks that don't have to be done by you when you're already working at full capacity. And for that you might need to brush up on your assertiveness skills.

BEING TREATED WITH RESPECT

Being assertive is about treating people equally and acknowledging your own right to be treated with respect and courtesy. They may be senior to you but you still have the right to be treated with respect – and if they aren't respectful then a few assertive techniques will quickly put them straight. Assertiveness isn't about aggression – far from it. It is about being confident enough to state your position and to get people to listen to you. It is about encouraging respect rather than demanding it. Assertive people are confident enough to be honest, to stand their ground and to have their opinion taken seriously.

Be honest

You are allowed to say what you think. It's as simple as that. This means that you can criticise people as long as you do it fairly and aren't rude or personal. You can begin by saying simply "I disagree" or "I don't think your idea is workable." It gets easier as you practise.

Stand your ground

Easy one this, just so long as you practise the scratched record technique. They want you to do something that you feel you can't do or that isn't appropriate. Easy. Just say "I'm afraid I can't do that." Then when they put the pressure on merely repeat "I'm sorry I can't do that." Just keep repeating it and they'll back down first. Assertiveness can be pretty intimidating in a nice way.

Get taken seriously

You have to express yourself in a calm and reasoned way. It's no good being unpleasant or confrontational. All you have to do is express yourself assertively by saying "I feel … when you…" This way you won't provoke any one but you will be taken seriously as in "I feel uncomfortable when you try and allocate extra work to me in public so that I can't discuss it properly with you."

Assertive behaviour doesn't get rid of all your problems but it can effectively deal with quite a lot that are caused by the so-called problem people – the ones that create problems by their behaviour being less than it should be in a modern civilised working environment.

One of the essentials of assertive behaviour is remaining calm at all times. Problem people often feed off others' anger, irritation or defensiveness. If you are calm, rational and confident there is simply nothing for them to gain. If they can't rile you they may leave you alone.

EXPRESSING HOW YOU FEEL

That doesn't mean you can't express your emotions. Letting someone know how you feel is fine but do it verbally, with words, rather than tears, hysteria, rage, punching or door slamming. It is so much more effective and productive to say "I feel very angry when you reprimand me in front of junior colleagues", rather than flouncing out of the office, sulking and slamming the door behind you. Both ways let the person know you are angry but saying it with words is so much more grown-up and will get much better results.

And if someone starts hurling abuse at you, it is very easy to get defensive and retaliate by shouting back. But it simply makes things worse. By remaining calm you stay focused. You keep a clear, objective perspective and can remain assertively in control. This gets you what you want quicker and more effectively. It is the smart approach.

Assertive feedback

The art of assertive feedback is to do it immediately, be clear, be honest and be respectful. So, if your manager tries to give you another job and you are at breaking point, give them the choice and make them decide what's most important: "I've got too much to do this week. If you'd like me to take on this new project, then the report I'm writing will have to shift back to next week. Which would you prefer me to do?".

ORGANISING YOUR TIME IN THE SWAMP

You might be able to reduce your overload by having a good look at how you spend your time and how effective you are. You have only a limited amount of time each day so it's best to be very clear about what you will spend or squander that time on. Cutting down the overload means setting goals and being realistic about them. It is also about valuing time – not wasting it on things you have no control over or can't change.

You're in the right

Remember – you know your working limits and if others are exceeding that limit you need to act, firmly and honestly. As long as you know you are working as effectively and efficiently as you can and are putting in the requisite hours, you have every right to say when you can't cope any more.

Swamp drainage

Key time-saving tactics

Here's a quick rundown on ideas for saving time:

- **Be organised.** Make and keep lists. Keep a filing system for everything – including household bills and tasks. Write down everything you need to know, remember, think about, plan and resource, on notepads. Keep a notepad with you at all times. As you think of things to do or remember, write them down.
- **Build in time off.** Into any plan build in breaks.
- **Don't do it all yourself.** Delegate as much as you can – it's not lazy, it's good time management.

- **Don't put it off**. Do it now – not tomorrow. Be ruthless about procrastination.
- **Find ways to speed things up**. Be on the lookout for ways to do things quicker – especially routine tasks that take up a lot of time and aren't very productive.
- **Have a clear picture** of what it is you are doing. Knowing what the end should be or look like is important. If you are working haphazardly you cannot be focussed.
- **Know when you work best**. Perhaps it's first thing in the morning; perhaps last thing at night. Whenever it is, allot tasks to that time that are important or difficult. Times when you know you work less well you can keep for less important or easier tasks.
- **Know your time**. Allocate the proportion of your time you think you should spend working, resting, socialising, playing and relaxing. Stick to it.
- **One task at a time**. Finish each thing before you move on to the next. Don't start anything unless you can finish it.
- **Plan time for yourself**. You are the brains behind the outfit – no matter what the outfit is (mainly yourself). Allow a little time each day for fun and enjoyment. This isn't laziness – it's healthy, therapeutic and essential. Without rest and relaxation the brain will seize up.
- **Prioritise your time**. Know how important each task is and do the most important first.

- **Schedule failure**. Allow a little time built into each task for disappointment, failure, being let down or having to delay. Then when things do go wrong you can cope.
- **Set deadlines.** Allot yourself time to finish tasks that is both realistic and attainable.

MANAGING STRESS AND OVERLOAD

Work can be stressful – but it can also be stimulating, challenging, motivating, creative, exciting, interesting, demanding and productive. Stress occurs when we are unable to cope with pressure. Pressure in itself isn't a bad thing. But what we all want is stimulating work, a pat on the back when we've done well, to keep our health and our sanity, and to have the right balance between work and life. Here are a few pointers:

- **Be strict** about weekends/evenings. This time is for you and your family if you have one (unless you're scheduled to work anyway, or choose to work then instead of during the day). Don't take work home or turn the computer on.
- **Be committed** to work while you're there and to home when you're not. If you aren't committed – change jobs; it's bad for you.
- **Eat sensibly.** And don't overdo the caffeine or alcohol.
- **Have a fixed working day** – and stick to it.
- **Have a life.** Don't spend all your time working, thinking about work, or talking about work. Have some friends

who don't work in the same business with whom you
can talk about different things.

- **Have goals**. Make sure your job furthers your life goals
  and that you aren't just filling in time waiting for
  something better to turn up.
- **Take breaks**. You need to get away from work every
  now and again. This might be every few hours, days,
  weeks or months but no one should expect you to
  work without suitable and beneficial breaks.

Interruption anybody?

Don't keep a free chair in your office/near your desk, or people will sit on it.
Once settled, the interruption will take twice as long. If you need a second
chair, keep some files on it and only remove them when you want someone
to sit down. If you're concentrating hard on a task, don't answer your
phone. Use your voicemail, or get someone to take messages.

Swamp drainage

- **Don't get too het up** about work. When all is said and
  done it's only a job. It might be very important to you
  but your health, happiness and welfare come first.
- **You are entitled to support**. If you need to retrain,
  develop new skills, improve, get help or even just talk
  about work problems, then you should be able to enlist
  support from the senior staff above you.

Richard Templar is the author of *The Rules of Work* and *Fast
Thinking Work Overload* (Prentice Hall Business).

Coaching yourself:
when it's you that needs to change – not the 'gators

You've probably worked out by now that this isn't all about alligators or swamps – being effective and happy at work largely depends on you. So, you may well have realised that there are bits of yourself you need to change – habits, behaviours, attitudes, whatever. And change isn't easy. A lot of us find that when we want to change a habit or behaviour that seems unhelpful or even damaging, we just can't seem to do it.

Some people seek help, through a counsellor, a personal trainer, a guru of some kind or other. Some try different kinds of therapies or courses, buy special "diet" food or nicotine patches, vow to go to the gym twice a week or get up earlier every morning. And every so often, despite all this effort the behaviour stays put. We accept our limitations and give up.

But some people do manage to make real, positive change in their lives. How do they do it?

There is no single secret, but there are a range of techniques that are proven to help people live a more purposeful, more fulfilling life. These techniques are used by life and business coaches, but if you don't have your own coach, you can still use some of these techniques to enhance your performance and productivity at home and at work.

UNDERSTANDING CHANGE

Change is not just a decision, it is a procedure, a cycle. Research has shown that for change to happen, we go through a clearly identifiable set of situations. Most of us spend a lot of time thinking about change before we actually take the plunge. Often we'll fail a few times before we succeed. Knowing that thinking about change, and even trying and failing is an important part of the change process, makes you much more likely to be able to deal with the uncertainty and ambiguity that change always brings with it.

Whatever the change – finding a new job, starting a new course, even starting a new relationship or leaving an unhappy one – you will find yourself at each stage weighing up the costs and benefits. When you get to the point where the benefits outweigh the costs then you'll probably make the change. Until that point change is difficult. Think about the costs and benefits and you'll feel more in control of the changes you are going through.

CREATING THE FUTURE

If you're going to make a huge change in your life, chances are you'll spend a lot of time thinking about it. When change is forced upon you (redundancy, for example) you need to spend time getting used to it. But when you decide for yourself to make a change, you're likely to have a long period of contemplation before you do anything about it. If you wanted to sail around the world, for example, you'd spend some time reading, thinking, researching, looking at different types of boat, and being generally interested in the idea. This means that when you finally decide to make a change in your life, whether it is your job, your home, or your relationship, you're usually further along the path of change than you might think.

Develop a fuzzy vision

Few of us know exactly what we want from life. Even if we're completely sure, life has a habit of intervening – and it may be that what you wish for is impossible or unattainable. It is unrealistic and limiting to develop too rigid a vision of the future. It's much more helpful to develop a "fuzzy vision" – an idea of the sort of life you want, the sort of area you want to be working in. This way you can be flexible and adapt to circumstances but stay on track.

One way to encourage yourself towards positive action is to imagine the future as you'd like it to be. A powerful technique for doing this is to write yourself a letter from the future. Choose a date sometime in the future, maybe a birthday or some other significant day, and write yourself a letter from that time. It could be a few months ahead or even a couple of years. It is important to write your thoughts down. Use all your senses to imagine how you would feel if things had been going well for you. By imagining the future, you give yourself clues as to what you really want, what is truly important to you. Chances are you've probably never done anything like this before and it might feel a bit odd or awkward. It might help to know that people from all backgrounds have not only done it, but found it very helpful; from top fighter pilots, to newsreaders, teachers and CEOs of large international organisations.

Planning a route

Once you've got some idea of the sort of future you would like to create for yourself, you can start to make some plans to get you there. You need to set yourself some goals – but make sure they're all SMART, i.e. Specific (goals aren't fuzzy), Measurable (you know when you've achieved them), Attractive, Realistic and Time-framed. You're much more likely to achieve them that way.

Motivating yourself

The key to motivation is simply to start. Take the first step – this is the most difficult one. Make it small, and promise yourself to do something small towards your goal every day.

Focus on solutions

We're often led to believe that we can only be happy if we deconstruct and understand everything that has happened to us. It can seem that unless we understand exactly why we behave as we do, we can never change it. It can be fascinating and very useful to understand the origins of the way you behave, but sometimes it is only once we have found a solution that we understand what the problem was. Coaching is "solution focused" – that is, instead of trying to fully understand the situation, it looks at how the world would feel if things were the way you wanted them to be. This is where the "Magic Question" comes in. Ask yourself "If I woke up tomorrow morning and my problem had completely disappeared, how would life feel? How would I know the problem had gone? How would other people know?" Start from there and then work your way towards that ideal scenario.

Gather resources

Most of us have some kinds of resources around us that we can draw strength from. It could be family, friends, books, music, a religious belief. Start using these resources. Consciously draw on these strengths to get you where you want to be. If you know what you want to change and where you want to be, give your project a name, and even choose a small symbol or talisman that you can carry around with you. Research shows that people who do this are more likely to succeed in their change projects.

6

Changing ANTs into PETs

No matter how well you plan your future, and how carefully you outline your goals, you may find that your unacknowledged, almost unconscious negative beliefs (Automatic Negative Thoughts) about yourself and the world can sabotage your best efforts. It's as though someone is sitting on your shoulder whispering, "You're no good", "You'll never make it", "You always fail". The problem with these negative thoughts is that we are often hardly aware of them, even though they can exert a powerful force over us. In order to defeat these thoughts you need to first identify them and then replace them with more positive thoughts (Performance-Enhancing Thoughts).

Alligators

Staying on track

Maybe you'll need to try several different approaches to change. Once you have set your goals there may well be different ways of reaching them. Your goals may even change along the way. You need to re-evaluate what you are doing and change what's not working. Try to anticipate problems and plan what you might do if they occur.

Accessing your goals

Schedule yourself a weekly GROW session where you look at your: **Goals** (Are they still realistic? Have they changed? Have you achieved any of them yet?); **Reality** (What's happened during the past week? What sort of problems have you encountered? How well did you deal with them, on a scale of 1 to 10? What worked? What didn't?); and **Options** (What is the full range of options available? Which of these are most attractive at the moment?). Then **Wrap up** (List some specific tasks. How will you know if you are being successful? Make a list of people who might help you achieve your aims. What will you do if you find things are getting in the way?).

Swamp drainage

Plan the future

Using these techniques, set yourself some targets and draw up an action plan for the next month. Make sure you do something towards your goal every day.

Celebrating success

It's very important that you take time to celebrate success, either on your own or with others. Record any milestones you reach along the way and allow yourself some time to feel good about your achievements.

Or, to put it even more simply: **How to Change Your Life**.

1. Work out what you want to change.
2. Choose an area to work on.
3. Understand that change is a process not just a decision.
4. Identify your needs and values. Work out what drives you.
5. Set yourself some SMART goals (Specific, Measurable, Attractive, Realistic, Time-framed).
6. Replace negative self-talk ("I can't do it") with performance-enhancing thoughts ("I've done it before").
7. Imagine your life where the problem has been solved. How does it look? Feel?
8. Give your project a name and a sign/symbol to represent it. Identify resources (physical, mental, emotional, spiritual, financial, situational) that can help you.
9. Develop an action plan. Small steps. Do something towards your goal each day. Record your progress. Do more of what is working, change what isn't.
10. Celebrate your success.

All these techniques are based on work done at the Coaching Psychology Unit, Department of Psychology, University of Sydney. The techniques are all scientifically validated. We know it works! Good luck.

Jane Grant and **Tony Greene** are authors of *Coach Yourself* (momentum).

Digging a bit deeper:
why care?

7

The critical moment came, as so often, in the dying minutes of a day-long conference, just as the coffee-diluted delegates were shuffling their papers in a homewards direction. A well-dressed man in his thirties – a former paratrooper – spoke from the back of the hall. "I took my platoon home to sample my mother's curry," he said. "When they'd gone, she asked me what I was to those men. I didn't know how to answer; 'their leader' was the best I could do. She then asked me what my first responsibility was to them. I said to protect them. But she said no, that wasn't right: 'You must, above all, love them.' She was right, I know – but this is the first time I've told this story, to anyone."

A paratrooper platoon leader seeing love as his primary workplace responsibility is an utterly counter-cultural, and therefore deeply moving, idea. That man held the audience like none of the platform speakers on that day. There were some looks of embarrassment (this was England, after all). But that young, old soldier brought to life a vision of a fuller, richer life at work. And for estate agents as much as paras – if our workers are our new neighbours, should we not love them?

WORK AS A BLESSING

It is all a far cry from the way most of us currently hold work in our lives, and in our collective consciousness. Work, the "sweat of our brow", is what Adam was condemned to, what criminals are condemned to – at best, what "pays the rent". We work to live, we proudly proclaim, not live to work. Work is still seen as a place of economic exchange: my labour for your money.

But it doesn't have to be like this. The truth is that good work – absorbing, meaningful work – is a blessing. More and more people are refusing to accept the false, economistic trade-off between "work" and "life", between their beliefs and the bottom line, between business and pleasure.

We spend more time in what Mihaly Csikszentmihalyi, a US psychologist, calls "flow" – absorption in a task so complete as to forget ourselves – at work than we do at leisure. Half of us meets our life partner in the office or on the shopfloor. Incresingly we say we want to work for a firm with a strong social commitment: the ethical employee is on the march.

There is a lot of talk in the management literature about bringing the "whole person" to work. This is laudable, but it won't happen by HR edict. It is ordinary women and men – you and me – who are the agents of change. And what we want is not just to look good at work, not just to do well, or even to be good – we want to *feel* good about our work.

Csikszentmihalyi, in a book called *Good Work*, co-written with Howard Gardner and William Damon, says: "The quality of life in the future will depend on whether we find a way to do good work… If the fundamentals of good work – excellence and ethics – are in harmony, we lead a personally fulfilling and socially rewarded life. If they are not, either the individual or the community, or both, will suffer."

Good work is about the quality of the work, certainly. I want the words I am writing now to communicate powerfully and eloquently. I want you to enjoy them. But I also want to think, to feel, that the presence of these words on this page has some chance of making the world just the tiniest bit better. *Mein Kampf* could have been well written (it wasn't), but it could never have been good work.

Good work is measured not in hours, or pounds, or cubic

> " *Work is still seen as a place of economic exchange: my labour for your money.* "

metres of office space, or prizes. It is measured by the feelings of the person engaged upon it. We know when we are proud of our work, when it says something glorious about ourselves, if only we let ourselves feel it. We also know when our work, no matter how "good" on the surface, how economically effective, how socially high in status, is bad work. Our work is one of the most important chapters in our life story – it shapes and defines us. If it is hollow, then ultimately it hollows us out, too. But there are so many pressures on us, on our time, our bank balances, our energy that it is too easy to stop listening to ourselves.

THE POST-MATERIALIST AGE

We are moving into a post-materialist age. This does not mean people do not want nice stuff: we will always want nice stuff. However, realisation is slowly dawning that stuff –

including money – is no longer making us happier. Money is losing some of its magic and some of its power to measure success. But we are struggling to find new benchmarks, new languages of advancement and growth. And work is at the centre of this change. We don't want to be wage slaves any more. We want wages, yes, but we want our work to be a better statement of our personal accounts.

Capitalism has been the undisputed engine of progress for centuries, and provides a framework for lots of useful activity. Of course capitalism has a long charge sheet: the creation of huge, ruthless multinationals; third-world debt; patriarchy; poverty; instability and so on. But to my mind the biggest charge against capitalism is its carelessness. By definition, capitalism is about things (capital, primarily, of course) rather than feelings or people. But care is what makes the world go round. We want to care about our work and take care over what we do at work, listening to our own and other's reactions; these are the currencies of the future.

Kahlil Gibran said that "work was love made visible" – a truth and a hope that the Hindi paratrooper had learned but then hoarded. Little by little the amount of good work being done, the amount of love becoming visible, can be increased. It is all about feeling good. And we only feel good when we give a damn. It starts here, today, with you.

Richard Reeves is the author of *Happy Mondays – Putting the Pleasure Back into Work* (momentum).

OSW is the largest co-ordinated guidance, training and employment programme for the homeless in Europe. A registered charity, we work through real partnerships to deliver training, education, advice and employment-related services for homeless people.

Working in partnership with a wide range of specialist education and training providers, OSW delivers services that engage homeless people in learning, prepare them for formal education or work and support them towards being successful in their chosen course or job.

Since 1999 we have:

- put over 1000 homeless people into jobs
- helped over 1000 access vocational training or further education
- helped over 1000 achieve qualifications
- had 4000 homeless people access our vocational services.

Recent developments include helping homelessness agencies across our partnership to develop top grade IT suites to give homeless people access to e-learning.

Through a small central team, we gain funding from European, National and Regional government structural funds, from the Community Fund and from charitable trusts.

For more information about OSW visit our website:
www.osw.org.uk

Get ahead; give a damn

"The Ant is strong when working individually and adaptable
when working in a team." Graham Pullen
Copyright Art Wolfe/www.artwolfe.com

ACKNOWLEDGEMENTS

With thanks to: the authors for sharing their wisdom; Carmel for
the phrase "have a job; give a damn" and for being the inspiration
she is; Waterstones for agreeing to sell this book and not take a
penny for it; Pearson plc for funding the project; Pearson Education
for use of resources; Kenny Grant for his huge generosity (jacket,
text design and typesetting all for free); Ashford Colour Press and
Precision Publishing Papers for the good deal on paper and
printing; finally big thanks to Michelle, Elie, Sarah, Rebecca,
Hermione, Felicity, Rod, Lesley, Magda, Melanie, Liz and Richard.

About the authors

Guy Browning is Creative Director of Smokehouse – an Innovation Consultancy – helping organisations from many different sectors brainstorm new products and services and new ways of working. His route to this was stand-up comedy, business failure, advertising, unemployment, monstrous blagging, serious job, leap into the unknown, jammy break.

Anthony Grant PhD is a Coaching Psychologist who works with organisations and individuals to improve their performance and their work/life experience. This no-nonsense, demonstrably effective solution-focused approach helps people to give a damn, to align their personal and work values, to build on existing resources, and to find a better way to live and work.

Jane Greene is a writer, editor and consultant specialising in lifelong learning. She believes that having a job and giving a damn makes sense not only for the individual but also for the organisation. Most people work best when they are working on something they believe in. Her book *Coach Yourself* uses techniques developed by Tony Grant at Sydney University and is designed to help you find out what you want to do with your life and how to start doing it.

Ros Jay is a professional writer and editor specialising in business topics. She writes almost exclusively for people who already have a job, and is delighted to be able to contribute to a book which will help people outside her usual readership: those who don't yet have a job. She lives in Devon with her husband and three young sons, whom she hopes will grow up both to get ahead and give a damn too.

Carmel McConnell Her background as a social activist taught her that in high-purpose, high-impact campaigns, the difference between success and failure is the quality of the team and the team working. In her case, the difference between getting an uninvited set of US cruise missiles (nukes) 60 miles west of London, or not, was down to the ability to harness the differences around the camp fire at Greenham Common. That was, of course, a very long time ago. In the 90 years since then she has trundled around the business environment and had a good, successful time using the same skills. She is now running a child poverty charity called Magic Sandwich, tackling inner city child malnourishment. Contact Carmel for more information on how you can help: carmelmcconnell@btinternet.com

Richard Reeves is a freelance journalist, writer, speaker and consultant. He was formerly Director of Futures at the Industrial Society (now the Work Foundation).

Rachael Stock is lucky enough to be the Publisher of all these brilliant and lovely authors. She wrote the introduction and edited the book.

Richard Templar is in work and firmly believes that all who are should put a bit back. Thus his contribution is entirely freely, willingly and happily given. He has learnt over many years, working as both a business manager and a business author, that there is a certain amount of luck in who works and who doesn't.